Based on the 2014
Computer Based Testing

DMV TEST

HOW TO PASS ON YOUR FIRST TRY

"A must have for teenagers who would like to pass on their first try!"

Written By:

FastTrackBooks.org

Over 200 Practice Problems!

- *Road Way Rules Test*
- *Traffic Signs Test*
- *Practical Questions*
- *Tips and Strategies*
- *Updated Test Questions*
- *Safety Tips*

TABLE OF CONTENTS:

The DMV Permit Test "How to Pass on Your First Try!" Over 200 practice test questions! A must-have for anyone who would like to pass on their first try. It is also great for any licensed driver who would like a refresher course on the latest traffic laws and road sign meanings. The thought of getting your driver's license can be a little bit intimidating, but with a few simple guidelines and test taking strategies, you'll be well on the road to success!

Our practice tests have **over 200** test questions and are an excellent way to prepare you for the actual written test. The book is split into two sections: The Traffic Signs Test (visual signs included) and The Road Way Test. Each test contains questions that are very similar to the actual test questions. By preparing, using these supplemental practice questions, as opposed to reading and rereading the DMV driver handbook which is very time consuming and can be a waste of time, you will learn basic driving skills, road sign and traffic signal meanings, when to pull over for emergency vehicles, speed limits in various zones, how to handle accidents, and much more. You will also learn how to answer the trick questions which appear time and time again on the test! Also included in the book are valuable test taking strategies, safe driving tips, and safe driver checklists.

Did you know that **70 percent** of first-time test takers **fail** the DMV permit test? Many people take their driving test and totally underestimate the level of difficulty of the questions. They do not sufficiently prepare, do not practice enough, and let their overconfidence get in the way. Others get very nervous because they don't know what to expect. Taking your driving permit test is the first step towards obtaining a driver's license. The entire process can be over whelming, but if you study, you will not have any problems passing it. Follow our simple steps to improve your chances of passing the permit test on your first try!

Passing the first time will save you money, time, and the stress of having to study again. It will also give you confidence and prepare you for the road driving test. With a little preparation and concentration, you can master the rules of the road and navigate your next driver's license test with confidence.

Good Luck!

Testing Strategy:

Set yourself up to pass your written driver's license test with these simple tips:

1) Prepare in advance weeks before the test. Read through the practice problems. Cramming the night before this test will only hurt you.

2) Get a good night's sleep before the exam.

3) Do not waste too much time on hard test questions. If you do not immediately know the answer, just skip it. You should try to solve the easy questions first. If you have time left, you should then go back to try to answer the harder questions.

4) Since the test is multiple choice, try to eliminate as many wrong answer choices as possible. If you can eliminate just one choice then you just increased your percentage of guessing correctly by almost 9%. If you can eliminate 2 wrong answer choices, then you just increased your percentage at guessing correctly by 25%!

5) Use common sense and do not over think the questions.

6) Do not leave any questions blank! Make an educated guess on every question.

7) You should study the road signs test and know it well enough to be able to see the sign and immediately recognize its meaning without looking at the possible answer choices.

8) Don't forget your paperwork! Before you rush out the door the morning of the test, be sure to grab the documentation and registration forms you will need.

9) Arrive early. Give yourself enough time to travel to the testing office. Rushing and being late will only make you nervous. Plan to arrive 15 minutes early and sit in your car and flip through this book on last time. Spend this time to relax and focus on the test questions.

10) Pay close attention to the numerical values in the handbook. These are often the hardest to remember, and many will be on the test.

Safe Driving Tips:

Practice these tips to improve your driving skills:

Do Not text while driving

Do Not talk on the cell phone while driving

Accelerate smoothly. Don't race the engine or make it stall.

Stop the vehicle gently. Start braking well ahead of where you must stop to avoid sudden "jerks."

Be sure your vehicle is in the correct gear. Don't grind the gears.

Always obey the posted speed limits. Remember to turn on your lights if you need to use your windshield wipers in poor weather conditions.

Follow at a safe distance. Use the three-second rule. Increase your following distance in bad weather or poor visibility.

Know what the traffic signals mean and obey them at all times.

Turn from the correct lane into the correct lane.

Signal for all lane changes and turns.

Know where to stop. Be aware of crosswalks. If your view is blocked at a crosswalk, move forward carefully and look both ways before entering the intersection.

Always look for potential hazards. Check your mirrors frequently

Steer smoothly at all times.

Always check your blind spot before changing lanes. Always look over your shoulder, do not trust your side mirrors.

Drive defensively. Anticipate another driver's errors.

Safe Driver Checklist:

Starting the Vehicle:

- Adjusts mirrors and seat
- Fastens safety belt

Stopping:

- Checks traffic
- Stops behind crosswalk or limit line.
- Stops without using accelerator at the same time.

Turns:

- Slows for turns.
- Begins and ends turns in the correct lane.
- Yields right of way when necessary.
- Sees and reacts to hazards.

Backing:

- Checks mirrors.
- Looks over right and left shoulder as appropriate.

Changing Lanes:

- Signals
- Checks mirrors.
- Checks over shoulder to view blind spot.
- Changes lanes safely.

Driving on the Freeway:

- Checks traffic flow.
- Signals early and slows on exit ramp.
- Adjusts speed to road conditions.

Defensive Driving Techniques:

- Checks mirrors before braking.
- Checks cross streets before passing.
- Checks signal lights and signs.
- Follows at a safe distance.

Traffic Signs Test:

1) What does the sign below indicate?

(A) This sign is made up and does not exist

(B) Narrow bridge ahead

(C) Wide roadway ahead

(D) Passing is illegal

2) What does the sign below indicate?

(A) This sign is made up and does not exist

(B) Cattle ranch is up ahead

(C) Cattle may be towed in this area

(D) Cattle may be crossing the road

3) What does the sign below indicate?

(A) Divided highway

(B) Railroad crossing

(C) An intersection of roads ahead

(D) Yield to oncoming traffic

4) What does the sign below indicate?

(A) No turning while the light is red even if the road is clear

(B) No turning while the light is red, only on a green arrow

(C) Turning is allowable from a two way road to a one way road

(D) None of the above

5) What does the sign below indicate?

(A) Look right and left for approaching traffic

(B) School zone ahead

(C) U-turn is permitted

(D) None of the above

6) What does the sign below indicate?

(A) Right lane ends

(B) Left lane ends

(C) Divided interstate highway

(D) Two lanes merge to one

7) What does the sign below indicate?

(A) Yield ahead

(B) Signal ahead

(C) Stop sign ahead

(D) School crossing ahead

8) What does the sign below indicate?

(A) Low clearance up ahead

(B) This sign does not exist

(C) Dip in the road ahead

(D) Drive In Precautionary mode (DIP)

9) The sign below is made up.

(A) True

(B) False

10) What does the sign below indicate?

(A) Yield to pedestrians

(B) Right turn is permitted

(C) Rail road crossing

(D) No passing

11) What does the sign below indicate?

Answer: _____?

12) What does the sign below indicate?

(A) Yield

(B) Hospital

(C) Stop

(D) Regulatory

13) What does the sign below indicate?

(A) No parking

(B) No praying

(C) Private access

(D) No parking except after 6pm on weekends

14) What does the sign below indicate?

(A) Yield

(B) School zone

(C) Regulatory

(D) Rail road crossing

15) When you approach this sign at an intersection, which way should you turn?

(A) Right

(B) Left

(C) Do not turn

(D) None of the above

16) Assume that you are driving at 35 miles per hour and you see the below sign up ahead. What does it mean?

(A) The exit up ahead is 25 mph

(B) There is a right curve up ahead in 25 miles

(C) There is a right curve coming up ahead which is at a 25 degree angle

(D) There is a right curve coming up ahead and the speed limit of 25 mph

17) White square or rectangular signs with white, red, or black letters or symbols, such as the one below, are usually what kind of signs?

(A) Regulatory

(B) Service

(C) Highway signs

(D) Warning

18) The sign below indicates which of the following?

(A) Yield

(B) Construction

(C) Regulatory

(D) Service

19) What does the sign below indicate?

(A) Speed limit of 80 mph

(B) State highway

(C) Interstate

(D) U.S. Highway

20) On a long car ride, you want to get out to stretch your legs. Should you pull over at this location?

(A) Yes

(B) No

21) What does the sign below indicate?

(A) You are approaching a one way highway or ramp from the correct direction

(B) You are approaching a two way highway or school from the wrong direction

(C) You are approaching a one way highway or ramp from the wrong direction

(D) You are approaching an illegal parking spot

22) What does the sign below indicate?

(A) One way in each direction

(B) No passing zone

(C) Undivided highway ahead

(D) Divided highway ahead

23) What does the sign below indicate?

DO
NOT
PASS

(A) Never pass

(B) Pass only when there is an emergency

(C) Pass on the left

(D) Passing is permitted

24) What does the sign below indicate?

(A) Ambulance could be entering the road ahead

(B) Fire truck could be entering the road ahead

(C) Trucks not allowed on this road

(D) Fire ahead

25) Square or rectangular signs with blue and white letters or symbols are what kind of signs?

(A) Service

(B) Warning

(C) Regulatory

(D) Route

26) What does the sign below indicate?

(A) Found on the back of an emergency vehicle

(B) Found on the back of a fast moving vehicle

(C) Found on the back of a slow moving vehicle

(D) Found on the back of a vehicle that frequency stops

27) What does the sign below indicate?

(A) Bicycle must follow the arrows

(B) Bicycle crossing only on left

(C) Bicycle must ride on left side

(D) Bicycle crossing

28) What does the sign below indicate?

(A) Moving vans can park here

(B) No truck zone

(C) Slow trucks entering the road

(D) Weight limit on trucks

29) What does the sign below indicate?

(A) Drunk drivers in area

(B) S-turn ahead

(C) Slippery when wet

(D) Truck spilled something on road

30) Which sign below means passing permitted?

   (A)   (B)   (C)   (D) None of these signs

31) What does the sign below indicate?

(A) Stop

(B) No passing

(C) Yield

(D) School zone

32) What does the sign below indicate?

(A) House ahead

(B) Yield

(C) Rail road crossing

(D) School crossing

33) What does the sign below indicate?

(A) Construction

(B) Informational

(C) Yield

(D) Regulatory

34) What does the sign below indicate?

(A) Speed limit sign of 65 miles per hour

(B) United States Highway sign

(C) United States Interstate sign

(D) Exit # 65

35) What does the sign below indicate?

(A) Guide or destination sign

(B) Warning sing

(C) Regulatory sign

(D) None of the above

36) What does the sign below indicate?

(A) Two way traffic

(B) Enter at your own risk

(C) No passing

(D) One-way road, do not enter

37) Put the signs above in proper order from left to right.

(A) Pass with care, construction, and yield

(B) School zone, construction, no passing

(C) Slow moving vehicle, no passing, and yield

(D) None of the above

38) What does the sign below indicate?

(A) This sign is 13 feet 6 inches high

(B) Be prepared to stop 13 miles ahead

(C) Keep 13 feet of distance to the vehicles in front of you

(D) Clearance ahead is 13 feet 6 inches high

39) What does the sign below indicate?

(A) Informational

(B) Regulatory

(C) Warning

(D) No passing

40) What does the sign below indicate?

(A) Do not enter

(B) Road ahead has a very sharp curve

(C) U turn is permitted

(D) No U turns

41) Square or rectangular signs with blue and white letters or symbols are what kind of signs?

(A) Service

(B) Regulatory

(C) Warning

(D) Informational

42) What does the sign below indicate?

(A) School crossing

(B) Rail road crossing

(C) Regulated roadway

(D) U turn ahead

43) What does the sign below indicate?

(A) Slow up but you can proceed if no cars are approaching

(B) Come to a rolling stop

(C) Come to a complete stop

(D) None of the above

44) What does the sign below indicate?

(A) Heliport

(B) No right turn

(C) High occupancy vehicles must turn right

(D) Hospital

45) Yellow diamond signs with black letters or symbols are what kind of signs?

(A) Warning

(B) Regulatory

(C) Reference

(D) Informational

46) What does the sign below indicate?

(A) Come to a complete stop

(B) Speed up to match traffic flow

(C) Slow down and be prepared to stop if necessary

(D) None of the above

Roadway Test:

47) It is okay to pass when approaching a curve or the top of a hill if you hurry.

(A) True

(B) False

48) What is one of the most important things to remember about driving at night or in fog?

(A) Drive within the range of your headlights

(B) Watch for cars at stop signs

(C) put on your hazard lights

(D) Use your high beams at all times

49) Which of the following is true about large trucks?

(A) They make wide right turns

(B) They take longer to stop than cars and motorcycles

(C) They tend to travel slower than other vehicles

(D) All of the above

50) Which of the following is a good example of defensive driving?

(A) Cleaning your mirrors before your drive

(B) Staying off of your cell phone

(C) Looking at the break lights on the car in front of you

(D) Looking for possible hazards

51) You can turn your vehicle while braking with ABS with less or no skidding than with regular brakes.

(A) True

(B) False

52) When turning from one of three turn lanes, which lane should you end up in after completing your turn?

(A) The outside lane

(B) The lane which has fewer cars in it

(C) The lane you started in

(D) The inside lane

53) What causes most rear end collisions?

(A) Texting

(B) Talking on cell phone

(C) Following too close

(D) Not checking your blind spot

54) Talking on a cell phone can increase your chances of being in a crash by as much as:

(A) It has the same chances

(B) Two times

(C) Three times

(D) Four times

55) Passing on the right is permitted when the driver of the other vehicle is making a left turn.

(A) True

(B) False

56) Where are ramp meters located?

(A) At the meter station

(B) On highway entrance ramps

(C) In middle lane of interstate

(D) On highway exit ramps

57) What is the correct left-turn hand signal?

(A) Hand and arm extended out at a 90 degree angle

(B) Hand and arm extended out the passenger side window

(C) Hand and arm extended out

(D) Hand and arm extended down

58) After drinking alcohol, you can lower your blood alcohol content by drinking coffee or taking a cold shower

(A) True

(B) False

59) When should you obey instructions from school crossing guards?

(A) Only during school hours

(B) Only if they present a license

(C) Only when children are present

(D) At all times

60) Pavement line colors indicate if you are on a one-way or two-way roadway.

(A) True

(B) False

61) Passing on the right is permissible but not ideal on one-way roads and streets and highways marked for two or more lanes of traffic moving in the same direction.

(A) True

(B) False

62) Passing is permitted in either direction if there are two solid yellow lines in the center of the road when?

(A) Passing is never permitted

(B) Only when following a slow vehicle

(C) Only during day time, not at night

(D) Only when it is safe

63) Which of the following are locations where you are likely to find slippery spots on the road?

(A) In tunnels or hilly areas

(B) In shady spots and on overpasses and bridges

(C) Near lakes

(D) On curbs at stop signs

64) Broken yellow lines separate lanes of traffic going in same direction:

(A) True

(B) False

65) You are driving and see a yellow sign. What does it mean?

(A) Special situation ahead

(B) School zone ahead

(C) Construction work ahead

(D) Federal interstate ahead

66) If you are driving at 50 miles per hour, how many feet will it take to react to an object in the road and stop your vehicle?

(A) 200 feet

(B) 300 feet

(C) 400 feet

(D) 500 feet

67) Which one of the following is the most important thing to remember about driving at night or in fog?

(A) Watch for pedestrians at intersections

(B) Be ready to honk your horn

(C) Drive below the posted speed limit

(D) Drive within the range of your headlights

68) Safety belts will never help you keep control of your car:

(A) True

(B) False

69) When should you signal if you plan to pull into a driveway just after an intersection?

(A) Before you cross the intersection

(B) In the middle of the intersection

(C) After you cross the intersection

(D) This is an illegal turn since it is near the intersection

70) Under which of the following situations can a driver use a handicapped parking space?

(A) If a handicapped person is in the vehicle when it is parked

(B) If the vehicle displays a handicapped person placard or license plate

(C) If a handicapped person is in the area when it is parked

(D) None of the above

71) Multiple lanes of travel in the same direction are separated by lane markings of what color?

(A) Yellow

(B) Red

(C) White

(D) Dashed yellow

72) While operating a motor vehicle, both hands should be on the steering wheel at all-times unless you are on the phone.

(A) True

(B) False

73) Is it ever lawful to drive faster than the posted speed limit?

(A) Yes, only when there is an emergency

(B) Yes, only when the car in front of you is driving too slow

(C) Yes, only when to keep up with the flow of other vehicles

(D) No, it is never lawful

74) When can you cross a solid yellow?

(A) To turn into a driveway if it is safe to do so

(B) To pass another vehicle on a state highway

(C) To make a U-turn on the interstate

(D) To try to get a glimpse of what is causing a traffic jam

75) A solid white line indicates what part of the traffic lane on a road?

(A) It combines lanes of traffic moving in opposite directions. Single white lines may also mark the right edge of the pavement

(B) It separates lanes of traffic moving in the same direction. Single white lines may also mark the left edge of the pavement

(C) It separates lanes of traffic moving in the same direction. Single white lines may also mark the right edge of the pavement

(D) It separates lanes of traffic moving in the same direction. Single white lines may also mark the right edge of the pavement

76) Which lane should you use if you are driving faster than other traffic on a freeway?

(A) The right lane

(B) The high occupancy vehicle (HOV) lane

(C) The middle lane

(D) The left lane

77) Generally, how far should you look ahead when driving on the highway?

(A) 2 - 3 seconds

(B) 5 - 10 seconds

(C) 10 -15 seconds

(D) 20 - 30 seconds

78) In which of the following conditions do you need extra following distance?

(A) When following trucks

(B) When driving on wet roads

(C) When visibility is limited

(D) All of the above

79) What should you do if you want to turn left at an intersection but oncoming traffic is heavy?

(A) Wait in the center of the intersection for traffic to clear

(B) Just start your turn because you have the right of way

(C) Wait in the left lane for traffic to clear

(D) None of the above

80) When are you permitted to cross an intersection with a flashing yellow light?

(A) Only after you come to a complete stop

(B) If you proceed with caution

(C) Only after you come to a complete stop and then speed through the light

(D) Only after you come to a complete stop and proceed not greater than 5 mph

81) When parallel parking, your wheels should be no more than how many inches from the curb?

(A) 18 inches

(B) 24 inches

(C) 36 inches

(D) 42 inches

82) When should low beams be used?

(A) In rain

(B) In darkness

(C) In foggy conditions

(D) None of the above

83) What is not true when it comes to large trucks and the road?

(A) They need more room to maneuver

(B) You should keep 5 seconds between you and the truck

(C) They have smaller blind spots than cars

(D) It takes them longer to stop

84) How many feet before your turn should you signal?

(A) 50 feet

(B) 100 feet

(C) 150 feet

(D) 200 feet

85) It is ok to pass another vehicle when approaching a curve or the top of a hill if you speed.

(A) True

(B) False

86) Which way should you turn your wheels if you park on an uphill grade?

(A) Left

(B) You should keep the wheels in the middle

(C) Right

(D) None of the above

87) A white X-shaped sign that says Railroad Crossing on it should be treated as a stop sign:

(A) True

(B) False

88) Which of the following places should you never park?

(A) In front of driveways

(B) Next to fire hydrants

(C) Pedestrian lanes

(D) All of the above

89) What is the minimum amount of feet that you must stop from a stopped school bus with its red lights flashing?

(A) 15 feet

(B) 20 feet

(C) 25 feet

(D) 30 feet

90) Lanes of traffic going in opposite directions are divided by what color lines?

(A) Yellow

(B) Orange

(C) Red

(D) White

91) When is it not legal to turn right at a red light?

(A) Only if there is a no-turn-on-red sign posted

(B) Only on one way roads

(C) It is always legal

(D) None of the above

92) During a skid, in what direction should you steer?

(A) In the direction of the skid

(B) Neither, you should slam on the brakes

(C) In the direction opposite of the skid

(D) None of the above

93) Under normal conditions, what is the minimum amount of a safe following distance?

(A) 1 second

(B) 2 seconds

(C) 4 seconds

(D) 8 seconds

94) It is okay not to make a full stop in which of the following situations?

(A) Flashing red

(B) Stop sign

(C) Red traffic light

(D) Flashing yellow

95) What should you do if your tire blows out?

(A) Apply the brakes and hold the steering wheel tightly

(B) Speed up and hold the steering wheel tightly

(C) Ease up on the gas pedal and apply the brakes

(D) Ease up on the gas pedal and hold the steering wheel tightly

96) You should yield to traffic on your right already in the roundabout.

(A) True

(B) False

97) What does keeping a steady speed and signaling well in advance when slowing down or turning help maintain?

(A) A safe distance in front of your vehicle

(B) A safe tire balance

(C) A safe distance behind your vehicle

(D) none of the above

98) What should you do if you are on a highway entrance and have to wait for a break in traffic before you can enter the roadway?

(A) Slow down on the entrance ramp to wait for a gap, and then sound your horn to alert drivers you are entering the roadway

(B) Slow down on the entrance ramp to wait for a gap, then speed up so you enter at the same speed that traffic is moving

(C) Slow down on the entrance ramp to wait for a gap, and then activate your emergency flashing lights to alert drivers you are entering the roadway

(D) Speed up and merge since you have the right of way

99) White square or rectangular signs with white, red, or black letters or symbols are which of the following type of signs?

(A) Informational

(B) Service

(C) Regulatory

(D) Direction

100) Which of the following is true about littering while driving?

(A) It is against the law

(B) It can cause an accident

(C) It could lead to jail time

(D) All of the above

101) What is the minimum safe following distance under most conditions?

(A) A minimum of 2 seconds is the recommended following distance under most conditions

(B) A minimum of 4 seconds is the recommended following distance under most conditions

(C) A minimum of 6 seconds is the recommended following distance under most conditions

(D) A minimum of 8 seconds is the recommended following distance under most conditions

102) Which of the following drugs can affect your ability to drive safely?

(A) Alcohol

(B) Marijuana

(C) Illegal drugs only

(D) Almost any drug can affect your ability to drive safety

103) What does a yellow sign mean?

(A) A special situation or hazard ahead

(B) School zone ahead

(C) Construction work ahead

(D) State highway ahead

104) What should you do if a railroad crossing has no warning devices?

(A) Speed up and then proceed with caution

(B) Slow down and then proceed with caution

(C) Every rail road crossing has a warning device

(D) Stop within 25 feet of the railroad crossing

105) Which vehicle has the right-of-way when more than one vehicle is stopped at an intersection?

(A) The first vehicle to arrive

(B) The last vehicle to arrive

(C) The vehicle on the right

(D) The vehicle on the left

106) What do white painted curbs mean?

(A) No parking zone

(B) No loading zone

(C) Loading zone for passengers or mail

(D) School zone

107) What should you do if you have a green light, but traffic is backed up into the intersection?

(A) Blow your horn to clear the intersection

(B) This is not your problem go around traffic

(C) Activate your emergency lights to clear the intersection

(D) Wait until traffic clears before entering the intersection

108) A driver turning left at an intersection must yield to what?

(A) Pedestrians, vehicles, and bicycles approaching from the right

(B) Pedestrians, vehicles, and bicycles approaching from the left

(C) Pedestrians, vehicles, and bicycles approaching from the opposite direction

(D) Pedestrians, vehicles, and bicycles approaching from the same direction

109) When driving in heavy fog during the daytime you should drive with your?

(A) Head lights on high beam

(B) Headlights off

(C) Hazard lights on

(D) Head lights on low beam

110) In which of the following situations is it ok to back up on the highway?

(A) To pick up a hitchhiker

(B) To check on an accident

(C) If you missed your exit

(D) It is never okay to back up on a highway

111) How fast may you legally drive when driving on a highway posted for 55 mph and the traffic is traveling at 65 mph?

(A) 65 mph

(B) No faster than 55 mph

(C) Between 55 mph and 65 mph

(D) Faster than 65 mph

112) Trying to go too fast from a stop can cause which of the following?

(A) Drive wheels to spin (peel out)

(B) Stuck gas pedal

(C) Brakes to fail

(D) Transmission problems

113) When should you obey a construction flagger's instructions?

(A) Only when the person is certified in flagging

(B) Only if he is wearing the proper barge to identify himself

(C) At no time in construction zones

(D) At all times in construction zones

114) If you miss your exit on a freeway it is legal to stop and back up on the shoulder:

(A) True

(B) False

115) What should you do if you are in an intersection and you hear a siren?

(A) Back up and pull over to the right side of the road and stop

(B) Stop and do not move until the emergency vehicle has passed

(C) Stop and do not move until you are instructed to do so

(D) Continue through the intersection, then pull over to the right side of the road and stop

116) What street sign does a flashing red signal light have the same requirements as?

(A) Stop sign

(B) Caution sign

(C) Yellow sing

(D) None of the above

117) How many seconds ahead should you focus in order to avoid danger?

(A) 5 - 10 seconds ahead

(B) 10 -15 seconds ahead

(C) 20 - 25 seconds ahead

(D) 30 -35 seconds ahead

118) In most states, what is true when it comes to sharing the road with bicyclists?

(A) Bicyclists have the same rights to use of public roads but follow rules designated in the Bicycle Handbook

(B) Bicyclists are not required to abide by all the same laws as regular vehicles

(C) Bicyclists are required to abide by all the same laws as regular vehicles

(D) None of the above

119) When driving behind a motorcycle, how much following distance should you allow?

(A) 8 seconds followings distance

(B) 4 feet

(C) 4 seconds followings distance

(D) 8 feet

120) By law, which passengers need to be wearing their safety belts in most states?

(A) Only the driver

(B) Only the passenger

(C) The driver and all front seat passengers in cars, vans, pickup trucks

(D) The driver and all back seat passengers in cars, vans, pickup trucks to be buckled up

121) If you are about to be hit from the back what should you NOT do?

(A) Brace yourself between the steering wheel and seat

(B) Press the back of your head firmly against head rest

(C) Brace yourself by putting your head between your knees

(D) Be ready to apply the brake

122) In most states, if you change your address, how long do you have to notify your motor vehicle office of the change?

(A) 5 days

(B) 20 days

(C) 15 days

(D) 10 days

123) How you will be able to identify a blind pedestrian? They are carrying which of the following?

(A) A red cane with a white tip

(B) A guide dog with a red collar

(C) A guide dog with a white collar

(D) A white cane with a red tip

124) When can you drive on the shoulder to pass a car?

(A) When the shoulder is big enough

(B) If traffic is really slow and your exit is in sight

(C) If the vehicle ahead of you is turning left

(D) Under no circumstance

125) What should you do when you are driving on the interstate and the vehicle in front of you is a large truck?

(A) Drive farther behind than you would for a passenger vehicle

(B) It depends on how big the truck is

(C) It depends on the weather conditions

(D) Drive same distance behind than you would for a passenger vehicle

126) When is it illegal to turn right at a red light?

(A) Only if there is a no school zone sign posted

(B) Only if there is a no-turn-on-red sign posted

(C) Only on two way roads slit by a dashed yellow line

(D) It is always legal

127) Which of the following practices are illegal to do while driving and are considered very dangerous?

(A) Reading a map

(B) Wearing headphones

(C) Talking on the phone

(D) Adjusting the outside mirror while the engine is on

128) When making a left turn from a two-way street to a one-way street in which lane should your vehicle be in when the turn is completed?

(A) In the middle lane

(B) In the left lane

(C) On the shoulder

(D) In the right lane

129) What is the best way to check your blind spot?

(A) Activate your vehicles camera which checks for you

(B) Just put on the turn signal and if a vehicle is there it will move

(C) Look over your shoulder

(D) It is impossible to check your blind spot

130) Why is night driving is more dangerous than driving in the day time?

(A) Traffic signs are less visible at night

(B) Pedestrians are less visible at night

(C) The distance we can see ahead is increased

(D) The distance we can see ahead is reduced

131) You can exceed the posted speed limit only when you are passing a group of cars:

(A) True

(B) False

132) Which of the following is a good idea to do on rainy, snowy, or foggy days at dusk, and when driving away from a rising or setting sun?

(A) Turn on the high beams

(B) Turn on the hazard lights

(C) Turn on the headlights

(D) Turn off the headlights

133) When a traffic signal light turns green, what should you do?

(A) Follow the 2 second rule

(B) Yield to pedestrians

(C) Do not move until you or instructed to move

(D) Speed up as quickly as possible

134) What does an orange sign mean?

(A) School zone ahead

(B) No passing ahead

(C) Rail road crossing ahead

(D) Construction work ahead

135) How many alcoholic drinks does it take to affect your driving?

(A) 1

(B) 2

(C) 3

(D) It is legal to driving while buzzed

136) It is legal to park next a fire hydrant as long as you as ready to move your vehicle:

(A) True

(B) False

137) looking and seeing events well in advance will help prevent which of the following?

(A) Panic stops

(B) Road rage

(C) Driver fatigue

(D) Drunk driving

138) Which of the following means to follow very close behind a vehicle?

(A) Drafting

(B) Following

(C) Spying

(D) Tailgating

139) You must use high beam lighting in fog, snow, and heavy rain.

(A) True

(B) False

140) When can roadways can become more hazardous to drivers?

(A) After it has been raining for several hours

(B) Right after it starts raining

(C) Right before it starts to rain

(D) After it has rained for 4 consecutive days

141) What should you do when parking on a downhill slope?

(A) By turning your wheels towards away the curb

(B) Just turn on the emergency brake

(C) By turning your wheels towards the curb

(D) Just turn on the emergency brake

142) When you back up in reverse in a passenger vehicle you should:

(A) Rely on your side mirrors

(B) Rely on your rear view mirror

(C) Rely on back up camera

(D) Look over your shoulder

143) What is the proper speed to travel when driving in adverse conditions?

(A) 50 mph

(B) The posted speed limit

(C) Only as fast as is safe to drive

(D) 65 mph

144) What is a safe following distance between your car and a car ahead under normal conditions?

(A) 2 seconds

(B) 50 feet

(C) 100 feet

(D) 10 seconds

145) How far are you required to stop from a school bus unloading children?

(A) 5 feet

(B) 55 feet

(C) 175 feet

(D) 30 feet

146) How far are you required to stop from an emergency vehicle?

(A) 175 feet

(B) 225 feet

(C) 500 feet

(D) 550 feet

147) What should you do when you arrive at a railroad crossing that does not have signals?

(A) Slow down and be prepared to stop

(B) Speed up and do not stop

(C) Come to a complete stop

(D) None of the above

148) Coffee, power aide, or a cold shower can lower your blood alcohol content after drinking alcohol:

(A) True

(B) False

149) Which of the following influence the effects of alcohol on the body?

(A) The person's weight

(B) The amount of alcohol consumed

(C) The amount of food in the stomach

(D) All of the above

150) You are not required to signal before you pull away from a curb or exit an interstate.

(A) True

(B) False

151) If you are about to get into a collision, it is better to swerve right instead of toward oncoming traffic:

(A) True

(B) False

152) Hitting a vehicle moving in the same direction is better than hitting a vehicle moving in the opposite direction

(A) True

(B) False

153) If your vehicle begins to skid you should?

(A) Press on accelerator and turn the steering wheel in the direction that you want the vehicle to go

(B) Ease off the brake and turn the steering wheel in the direction that you want the vehicle to go

(C) Ease off the brake and turn the steering wheel in the opposite direction that you want the vehicle to go

(D) Press on accelerator and turn the steering wheel in the opposite direction that you want the vehicle to go

154) If you are traveling 33 mph on a highway with a speed limit of 50 mph, which lane should you be in?

(A) Far left lane

(B) Shoulder

(C) Middle lane

(D) Far right lane

155) What should you do when the police are directing you to drive through a red light?

(A) Always obey the traffic signals first

(B) Pull over and stop until further instructions

(C) Drive through the red light

(D) Stop if the signal light turns red

156) It is sometimes legal to double park?

(A) True

(B) False

157) Which of the following does not affect braking distance?

(A) Width of the vehicle

(B) Tire conditions

(C) Road conditions

(D) Weight of the vehicle

158) What should you do if your gas pedal gets stuck?

(A) Keep your eyes on the road, quickly shift to neutral, stay in your current lane, and turn off the engine

(B) Keep your eyes on the road, quickly shift to neutral, pull off the road when safe to do so and turn off the engine

(C) Keep your eyes on the road, quickly shift to neutral, text someone for help, and turn off the engine

(D) Quickly shift to neutral, pull off the road immediately regardless of other vehicles, and turn off the engine

159) You may cross a double yellow line to pass another vehicle if the yellow line next to you is what?

(A) A dashed line

(B) A thicker line

(C) A broken line

(D) None of the above

160) It is legal to drive a vehicle in a bicycle lane when:

(A) It is never legal

(B) If your hazard lights are activated

(C) If you honk your horn first

(D) For less than 200 feet when preparing to turn

161) What is the definitions of a blind spot?

(A) Blind spots are areas near the front and rear of your vehicle that you cannot see in your rearview mirrors

(B) Blind spots only occur at night when an oncoming vehicle shines its lights into your eyes

(C) Blind spots refer to driver who have been drinking alcohol

(D) Blind spots are areas near the left and right rear corners of your vehicle that you cannot see in your rearview mirrors

162) What should you do if another vehicle is following you too closely?

(A) If there is enough room, just move into another lane

(B) Slow down slowly

(C) Accelerate so they don't hit you

(D) Honk your horn

163) The best thing you can do is to apply the brakes firmly if your car starts to skid:

(A) True

(B) False

164) You may cross a double yellow line to pass another vehicle if the yellow line next to you is what?

(A) Thinner line

(B) Broken line

(C) Thicker line

(D) None of the above

165) When should safety belts be worn?

(A) Only when riding in the front seat

(B) Only if you see a police officer

(C) At all times as a driver and as a passenger

(D) Only if driving faster than 55 mph

166) If you are driving with your high beams on and an oncoming vehicle approaches, how many feet in advance must you dim your lights?

(A) 400 feet

(B) 450 feet

(C) 500 feet

(D) 550 feet

167) If you are carrying a load that extends four or more feet past the bed of your truck, what color and what shaped flag must be attached to the rear of the load?

(A) A square, red flag

(B) A circular, green flag

(C) A square, green flag

(D) A circular, red flag

168) Eating, drinking, angry, ill, and texting are all examples of this kind of driving?

(A) Defensive

(B) Distracted

(C) Safe

(D) Offensive

169) Which of the following vehicles must stop at railroad crossings?

(A) 18- wheelers

(B) School buses

(C) School buses and passenger buses

(D) All vehicles

170) If there is another lane open, it is ok to continue at the same speed if an emergency vehicle is approaching you with a siren and flashing lights.

(A) True

(B) False

171) When can you legally block an intersection?

(A) Only during rush hour

(B) You cannot legally block an intersection

(C) Only when the light is yellow

(D) Only when other cars allow you

172) When you pass a vehicle traveling in the same direction, you should pass on the right.

(A) True

(B) False

173) When can you make a left turn at a green light?

(A) Only if there is a green turn arrow

(B) Only if there is a posted sign which allows you

(C) Only if you yield to oncoming traffic

(D) Only on one way streets

174) It is illegal to pass another vehicle stopped for pedestrians in a crosswalk.

(A) True

(B) False

175) At which of the following speeds can you can lose all traction and start hydroplaning?

(A) 30 mph

(B) 40 mph

(C) 50 mph

(D) 60 mph

176) Multiple lanes of travel in the same direction are separated by lane markings of what color?

(A) White

(B) Yellow

(C) Red

(D) Orange

177) How many feet before your intended turn should you signal?

(A) 15 feet

(B) 75 feet

(C) 100 feet

(D) 175 feet

178) What should you do when approaching a road construction work zone?

(A) Prepare to call someone since you will be bored in traffic

(B) Prepare to speed up

(C) Prepare to activate your hazard lights

(D) Prepare to slow down

179) The correct way to enter a freeway smoothly is to slow down on the entrance ramp to wait until a gap appears in the freeway traffic in the right lane.

(A) True

(B) False

180) How many times should you increase your following distance on a wet roadway?

(A) 1 time

(B) 2 times

(C) 3 times

(D) 4 times

181) When approaching an intersection with traffic control signals that are not working, you should treat it as you would a 4-way stop sign.

(A) True

(B) False

182) Unless prohibited by a sign, when may you turn left at a red light?

(A) From a one way road to a two way road

(B) From a two way road to a one way road

(C) From a two way road to a two way road

(D) From a one way road to a one way road

183) Quickly tapping your brake pedal 3 or 4 times can help let those driving behind you know that you are about to slow down.

(A) True

(B) False

184) When you merge with traffic, you should try to enter traffic at what speed?

(A) Faster speed than traffic

(B) Slower speed than traffic

(C) The same speed as traffic

(D) None of the above

185) You are not required to make a full stop in which of the following situations?

(A) At a flashing red traffic signal

(B) At a flashing yellow traffic signal

(C) At a stop sign

(D) At a red traffic light

186) The state examiner will check the person's vehicle before beginning the driving test to:

(A) Make sure that the vehicle is equipped with a hands free device for cell phones

(B) Make sure that the vehicle is in safe operating condition

(C) Check for cleanliness

(D) None of the above

187) Different rules apply as for maneuvering through any other type of intersection when driving a roundabout.

(A) True

(B) False

188) A solid or dashed yellow line indicates the left edge of traffic lanes going in your direction.

(A) True

(B) False

189) It is ok to continue at the same speed if an emergency vehicle is approaching you with a siren and flashing lights if there is another lane open.

(A) True

(B) False

190) Motorcycles can stop as quickly as other vehicles.

(A) True

(B) False

191) Which of the following emotions can have a great effect on your ability to drive safely?

(A) Worried

(B) Anger

(C) Excited

(D) All of the above

192) Driving much slower than the speed limit in normal conditions can do what?

(A) It can decrease the chance of an accident

(B) It doesn't do anything

(C) Help make you a better driver

(D) It can increase the chance of an accident

193) Pavement line colors do not indicate if you are on a one-way or two-way roadway.

(A) True

(B) False

194) You must never pass on the right if it means driving off the paved or main portion of the roadway.

(A) True

(B) False

195) Lanes of traffic going in opposite directions are divided by what color lines?

(A) White

(B) Red

(C) Yellow

(D) Red

196) When experiencing glare from a vehicles headlights at night you should?

(A) Look toward the right edge of your lane

(B) Look toward the left edge of your lane

(C) Look toward the front of your car

(D) Look toward the floor

197) You should use your horn to alert drivers that they have made an error.

(A) True

(B) False

198) How far ahead should you look when you are driving in town?

(A) 1 quarter mile

(B) 1 city block

(C) 1 mile

(D) 1000 feet

199) What does a red painted curb mean?

(A) No passing

(B) No loading

(C) Reserved for drop off

(D) No parking or stopping

200) Passing is permitted in either direction if there are two solid yellow lines in the center of the road when?

(A) When following a slow truck

(B) Passing is never permitted

(C) When it is safe to pass

(D) When following a slow vehicle

201) Talking on a cell phone can increase your chances of being in a crash by as much as four times.

(A) True

(B) False

202) If you see an oncoming car approaching in your lane you should:

(A) Flash your lights

(B) Honk your horn

(C) Pull off the right and slow down

(D) All of the above

Traffic Signs Test # 1: (Solutions)

Solution to Question # 1:

(B) Narrow bridge ahead

Solution to Question # 2:

(D) Cattle may be crossing the road

Solution to Question # 3:

(C) An intersection of roads ahead

Solution to Question # 4:

(A) No turning while the light is red even if the road is clear

Solution to Question # 5:

(D) None of the above

Solution to Question # 6:

(A) Right lane ends

Solution to Question # 7:

(B) Signal ahead

Solution to Question # 8:

(C) Dip in the road ahead

Solution to Question # 9:

(B) False

Solution to Question # 10:

(D) No passing

Solution to Question # 11:

School zone

Solution to Question # 12:

(C) Stop

Solution to Question # 13:

(A) No parking

Solution to Question # 14:

(D) Rail road crossing

Solution to Question # 15:

(B) Left

Solution to Question # 16:

(D) There is a right curve coming up ahead and the speed limit of 25 mph

Solution to Question # 17:

(A) Regulatory

Solution to Question # 18:

(B) Construction

Solution to Question # 19:

(D) U.S. Highway

Solution to Question # 20:

(B) No. It is not recommended to stop at this location.

Solution to Question # 21:

(C) You are approaching a one way highway or ramp from the wrong direction

Solution to Question # 22:

(D) Divided highway ahead

Solution to Question # 23:

(A) Never pass

Solution to Question #24:

(B) Fire truck could be entering the road ahead

Solution to Question # 25:

(A) Service

Solution to Question # 26:

(C) Found on the back of a slow moving vehicle

Solution to Question #27:

(D) Bicycle crossing

Solution to Question # 28:

(C) Slow trucks entering the road

Solution to Question #29:

(C) Slippery when wet

Solution to Question # 30:

(D) None of these signs

Solution to Question # 31:

(C) Yield

Solution to Question #32:

(D) School crossing

Solution to Question # 33:

(B) Informational

Solution to Question # 34:

(C) United States Interstate sign

Solution to Question #35:

(A) Guide or destination sign

Solution to Question # 36:

(D) One-way road, do not enter

Solution to Question # 37:

(C) Slow moving vehicle, no passing, and yield

Solution to Question #38:

(D) Clearance ahead is 13 feet 6 inches high

Solution to Question # 39:

(B) Regulatory

Solution to Question # 40:

(D) No U turns

Solution to Question #41:

(A) Service

Solution to Question # 42:

(B) Rail road crossing

Solution to Question #43:

(C) Come to a complete stop

Solution to Question #44:

(D) Hospital

Solution to Question #45:

(A) Warning

Solution to Question #46:

(C) Slow down and be prepared to stop if necessary

Roadway Test Solutions:

Solution to Question #47:

(B) False

Solution to Question #48:

(A) Drive within the range of your headlights

Solution to Question #49:

(D) All of the above

Solution to Question #50:

(D) Looking for possible hazards

Solution to Question #51:

(A) True

Solution to Question #52:

(C) The lane you started in

Solution to Question #53:

(C) Following too close

Solution to Question #54:

(D) Four times

Solution to Question #55:

(A) True

Solution to Question #56:

(B) On highway entrance ramps

Solution to Question #57:

(C) Hand and arm extended out

Solution to Question #58:

(B) False

Solution to Question #59:

(D) At all times

Solution to Question #60:

(A) True

Solution to Question #61:

(A) True

Solution to Question #62:

(A) Passing is never permitted

Solution to Question #63:

(B) In shady spots and on overpasses and bridges

Solution to Question #64:

(B) False

Solution to Question #65:

(A) Special situation ahead

Solution to Question #66:

(C) 400 feet

Solution to Question #67:

(D) Drive within the range of your headlights

Solution to Question #68:

(B) False

Solution to Question #69:

(C) After you cross the intersection

Solution to Question #70:

(B) If the vehicle displays a handicapped person placard or license plate

Solution to Question #71:

(C) White

Solution to Question #72:

(B) False

Solution to Question #73:

(D) No, it is never lawful

Solution to Question #74:

(A) To turn into a driveway if it is safe to do so

Solution to Question #75:

(D) It separates lanes of traffic moving in the same direction. Single white lines may also mark the right edge of the pavement

Solution to Question #76:

(D) The left lane

Solution to Question #77:

(C) 10 -15 seconds

Solution to Question #78:

(D) All of the above

Solution to Question #79:

(A) Wait in the center of the intersection for traffic to clear

Solution to Question #80:

(B) If you proceed with caution

Solution to Question #81:

(A) 18 inches

Solution to Question #82:

(C) In foggy conditions

Solution to Question #83:

(C) They have smaller blind spots than cars

Solution to Question #84:

(B) 100 feet

Solution to Question #85:

(B) False

Solution to Question #86:

(A) Left

Solution to Question #87:

(B) False

Solution to Question #88:

(D) All of the above

Solution to Question #89:

(B) 20 feet

Solution to Question #90:

(A) Yellow

Solution to Question #91:

(A) Only if there is a no-turn-on-red sign posted

Solution to Question #92:

(C) In the direction opposite of the skid

Solution to Question #93:

(C) 4 seconds

Solution to Question #94:

(D) Flashing yellow

Solution to Question #95:

(D) Ease up on the gas pedal and hold the steering wheel tightly

Solution to Question #96:

(B) False

Solution to Question #97:

(C) A safe distance behind your vehicle

Solution to Question #98:

(B) Slow down on the entrance ramp to wait for a gap, then speed up so you enter at the same speed that traffic is moving

Solution to Question #99:

(C) Regulatory

Solution to Question #100:

(D) All of the above

Solution to Question #101:

(B) A minimum of 4 seconds is the recommended following distance under most conditions

Solution to Question #102:

(D) Almost any drug can affect your ability to drive safety

Solution to Question #103:

(A) A special situation or hazard ahead

Solution to Question #104:

(B) Slow down and then proceed with caution

Solution to Question #105:

(A) The first vehicle to arrive

Solution to Question #106:

(C) Loading zone for passengers or mail

Solution to Question #107:

(D) Wait until traffic clears before entering the intersection

Solution to Question #108:

(C) Pedestrians, vehicles, and bicycles approaching from the opposite direction

Solution to Question #109:

(D) Head lights on low beam

Solution to Question #110:

(D) It is never okay to back up on a highway

Solution to Question #111:

(B) No faster than 55 mph

Solution to Question #112:

(A) Drive wheels to spin (peel out)

Solution to Question #113:

(D) At all times in construction zones

Solution to Question #114:

(B) False

Solution to Question #115:

(D) Continue through the intersection, then pull over to the right side of the road and stop

Solution to Question #116:

(A) Stop sign

Solution to Question #117:

(B) 10 -15 seconds ahead

Solution to Question #118:

(C) Bicyclists are required to abide by all the same laws as regular vehicles

Solution to Question #119:

(C) 4 seconds followings distance

Solution to Question #120:

(C) The driver and all front seat passengers in cars, vans, pickup trucks

Solution to Question #121:

(A) Brace yourself between the steering wheel and seat

Solution to Question #122:

(D) 10 days

Solution to Question #123:

(D) A white cane with a red tip

Solution to Question #124:

(D) Under no circumstance

Solution to Question #125:

(A) Drive farther behind than you would for a passenger vehicle

Solution to Question #126:

(B) Only if there is a no-turn-on-red sign posted

Solution to Question #127:

(B) Wearing headphones

Solution to Question #128:

(B) In the left lane

Solution to Question #129:

(C) Look over your shoulder

Solution to Question #130:

(D) The distance we can see ahead is reduced

Solution to Question #131:

(B) False

Solution to Question #132:

(C) Turn on the headlights

Solution to Question #133:

(B) Yield to pedestrians

Solution to Question #134:

(D) Construction work ahead

Solution to Question #135:

(A) 1

Solution to Question #136:

(B) False

Solution to Question #137:

(A) Panic stops

Solution to Question #138:

(D) Tailgating

Solution to Question #139:

(B) False

Solution to Question #140:

(B) Right after it starts raining

Solution to Question #141:

(C) By turning your wheels towards the curb

Solution to Question #142:

(D) Look over your shoulder

Solution to Question #143:

(C) Only as fast as is safe to drive

Solution to Question #144:

(A) 2 seconds

Solution to Question #145:

(D) 30 feet

Solution to Question #146:

(C) 500 feet

Solution to Question #147:

(A) Slow down and be prepared to stop

Solution to Question #148:

(B) False

Solution to Question #149:

(D) All of the above

Solution to Question #150:

(B) False

Solution to Question #151:

(A) True

Solution to Question #152:

(A) True

Solution to Question #153:

(B) Ease off the brake and turn the steering wheel in the direction that you want the vehicle to go

Solution to Question #154:

(D) Far right lane

Solution to Question #155:

(C) Drive through the red light

Solution to Question #156:

(B) False

Solution to Question #157:

(A) Width of the vehicle

Solution to Question #158:

(B) Keep your eyes on the road, quickly shift to neutral, pull off the road when safe to do so and turn off the engine

Solution to Question #159:

(C) A broken line

Solution to Question #160:

(D) For less than 200 feet when preparing to turn

Solution to Question #161:

(D) Blind spots are areas near the left and right rear corners of your vehicle that you cannot see in your rearview mirrors

Solution to Question #162:

(A) If there is enough room, just move into another lane

Solution to Question #163:

(B) False

Solution to Question #164:

(B) Broken line

Solution to Question #165:

(C) At all times as a driver and as a passenger

Solution to Question #166:

(C) 500 feet

Solution to Question #167:

(A) A square, red flag

Solution to Question #168:

(B) Distracted

Solution to Question #169:

(C) School buses and passenger buses

Solution to Question #170:

(B) False

Solution to Question #171:

(B) You cannot legally block an intersection

Solution to Question #172:

(B) False

Solution to Question #173:

(C) Only if you yield to oncoming traffic

Solution to Question #174:

(A) True

Solution to Question #175:

(C) 50 mph

Solution to Question #176:

(A) White

Solution to Question #177:

(C) 100 feet

Solution to Question #178:

(D) Prepare to slow down

Solution to Question #179:

(B) False

Solution to Question #180:

(B) 2 times

Solution to Question #181:

(A) True

Solution to Question #182:

(D) From a one way road to a one way road

Solution to Question #183:

(A) True

.

Solution to Question #184:

(C) The same speed as traffic

Solution to Question #185:

(B) At a flashing yellow traffic signal

Solution to Question #186:

(B) Make sure that the vehicle is in safe operating condition

Solution to Question #187:

(B) False

Solution to Question #188:

(A) True

Solution to Question #189:

(B) False

Solution to Question #190:

(A) True

Solution to Question #191:

(D) All of the above

Solution to Question #192:

(D) It can increase the chance of an accident

Solution to Question #193:

(B) False

Solution to Question #194:

(A) True

Solution to Question #195:

(C) Yellow

Solution to Question #196:

(A) Look toward the right edge of your lane

Solution to Question #197:

(B) False

Solution to Question #198:

(B) 1 city block

Solution to Question #199:

(D) No parking or stopping

Solution to Question #200:

(B) Passing is never permitted

Solution to Question #201:

(A) True

Solution to Question #202:

(D) All of the above

33400159R10062

Made in the USA
San Bernardino, CA
23 April 2019